The Christian Idea of Man

Other works by Josef Pieper from St. Augustine's Press

The Concept of Sin

Death and Immortality

Enthusiasm and Divine Madness: On the Platonic Dialogue Phaedrus

Happiness and Contemplation

In Tune with the World: A Theory of Festivity

Not Yet the Twilight (2nd in his autobiography trilogy)

The Platonic Myths

Scholasticism: Personalities and Problems of Medieval Philosophy

The Silence of St. Thomas: Three Essays

The Silence of Goethe

Tradition: Concept and Claim

Tradition as Challenge

What Catholics Believe (with Heinz Kastop)

Other titles of interest

C.S. Lewis and Don Giovanni Calabria, *The Latin Letters of C.S. Lewis*

Servais Pinckaers, O.P., *Morality: The Catholic View*

Peter Kreeft, *The Philosophy of Jesus*

Peter Kreeft, *Jesus-Shock*

Thomas Aquinas, *Treatise on Law*

Thomas Aquinas, *Treatise on Human Nature*

Thomas Aquinas, *Commentary on Aristotle's Nicomachean Ethics*

Thomas Aquinas, *Disputed Questions on Virtue*

St. Augustine, *On Order [De Ordine]*

Robert Hugh Benson, *Lord of the World*

James V. Schall, *The Regensburg Lecture*

The Christian Idea of Man

Josef Pieper

Preface by John Haldane
Translated by Dan Farrelly

ST. AUGUSTINE'S PRESS
South Bend, Indiana

Manufactured in the United States of America

2 3 4 5 6   20 19 18 17 16 15 14

Library of Congress Cataloging in Publication Data
Pieper, Josef, 1904–1997.
[Über das christliche Menschenbild. English]
The Christian idea of man / Josef Pieper;
preface by John Haldane; translated by Dan Farrelly.
p. cm.
Originally published in German with title: Über das
christliche Menschenbild. Munich: Kösel-Verlag.
Includes index.
ISBN 978-1-58731-111-6 (hardbound: alk. paper) –
ISBN 978-1-58731-112-3 (paperbound: alk. paper)
1. Virtues. 2. Christian ethics – Catholic authors.
3. Theological anthropology – Catholic Church. I. Title.
B3323.P433U2213 2011
233 – dc22   2011008091

ST. AUGUSTINE'S PRESS
www.staugustine.net

Contents

Preface

THE PUBLICATION OF THE PRESENT SHORT WORK IN A
new translation is very welcome. It makes avail-
able an early formulation of some of Pieper's central arguments about the structure and role of
virtue, together with his criticism of certain conceptions of the ethical and its relation to human
happiness. These conceptions had long prevailed
up to the period before, during, and after the
Second World War when Pieper was thinking and
writing about the nature of virtue; and they
remain with us today, notwithstanding the rise of
what has come to be called "virtue ethics."

The Christian Idea of Man was first published
in English as the opening essay of the January
1949 number of the quarterly journal *The
Review of Politics*. The *Review* had been founded
ten years previously at the University of Notre
Dame by Waldemar Gurian. Born into an affluent
Jewish family in Russia in 1902, Gurian moved to
Germany with his mother and sister prior to the
start of the First World War, and there they all

entered the Catholic Church. Thereafter he was educated in Cologne, Breslau, Munich, and Berlin, working with Max Scheler on a Ph.D. thesis on the Catholic youth movement, and mixing with other Catholic intellectuals.

In 1937, with the Second World War in prospect, Gurian emigrated, this time to the U.S., where he entered the company of a variety of important American and European emigré intellectuals, including Jacques Maritain, Hannah Arendt, Eric Voegelin, and Yves Simon. In Germany Gurian had edited the *Cologne People's Daily* and once in America was eager to apply his knowledge and skills to the task of creating a Catholic cultural and political journal. The *Review of Politics* provided a forum in which those named and others could reflect on the decline of Western civilization and consider how it might be rebuilt after the ravages of European revolutions, pogroms and wars. Against that background it was appropriate also to draw in writings by others who had remained behind in Europe though they shared the same concerns about its moral collapse.

Such is the background to the previous English publication of Pieper's *Christian Idea of Man*. The availability of a new edition, translated afresh, should be welcome both to scholars and to general readers interested in its themes, for it provides a clear account of the way in which Pieper brought together what had hitherto been interests in separate virtues, and of how he saw these as standing in need of a philosophical and theological anthropology. Arguably, today we stand in even greater need of an understanding of the relation of norms and values to our shared human nature and our common human destiny.

Although short, Pieper's essay contains a great deal to be thought about and discussed. Anyone familiar with recent moral philosophy and theology should be struck by how it anticipates two themes which have loomed large in those disciplines since the 1980s: namely, the need to find an important place in ethics for virtue, and the charge that liberalism is an expression of an individualism that shows little interest in, and may even be incapable of acknowledging, an irreducible common good.

In 1958, a decade after the first English translation of *The Christian Idea*, the British philosopher Elizabeth Anscombe published a revolutionary essay in *Philosophy* (the journal of the Royal Institute of Philosophy) under cover of the rather prosaic title "Modern Moral Philosophy." In this she presented three theses. First, that moral philosophy, as it was then conceived and practiced, needed to be set aside until an adequate philosophy of psychology was developed. Second, that the distinctively commandatory notions of moral obligation, duty and prohibition, should also be set to one side if not, perhaps, entirely abandoned. Third, that moral philosophers from Henry Sidgwick (1838–1900) to the time of Anscombe's essay all favored pretty much the same, disastrous, view.

Sidgwick was the author a major work entitled *The Methods of Ethics* (1874), which the American philosopher John Rawls described as "the clearest and most accessible formulation of what we may call 'the classical utilitarian doctrine' [namely that] the ultimate moral end of social and individual action is the greatest net sum of the happiness of all sentient beings." Anscombe, however, located his utilitarianism within a broader style of thought, which she saw as emerging with Sidgwick but as then characterizing all subsequent English moral philosophy, and which she named "consequentialism," thereby introducing a new word to the English language and a new concept to philosophy.

Allowing for differences of context, style, and

emphasis, the two essays by Anscombe and Pieper can be seen to be partly convergent and generally complementary. Both are agreed that prevalent notions of morality, as a system of rules consisting of sets of obligations and prohibitions, are distractions from the primary business, which is that of living a good life, and both present the idea of virtue as more fruitful and as introducing the need to relate the question of how to live to the nature of the being whose life is in question. As Anscombe puts it, "It might remain to look for 'norms' in human virtues . . . perhaps the species man, regarded not just biologically, but from the point of view of the activity of thought and choice with regard to the various departments of life – powers and faculties and use of things needed 'has' such-and-such virtues: and this 'man' with the complete set of virtues is the 'norm.'"

As if in response Pieper makes the same point but then indicates the need to carry the business forward beyond philosophy to theology. He writes, in commenting on Aquinas: "people should not think so much about what they ought to do, they should think about what they ought to be. . . . that is the first teaching of the 'Doctor Communis': ethics is about the right conception of man. Naturally it is also concerned with doing, duties, commandments, and sins. But its primary object, which is the foundation of everything else, is: man's proper existence, the image of the good person." Apt to her philosophical purpose, Anscombe stops short, keeping her idealized agent within the domain of nature; but she would not have objected to the move to the supernatural order so as an enlarged theologized anthropology is concerned, indeed she would have insisted upon it. Pieper introduces that religious ideal, but immediately connects it to an ontological reality. He writes: "The answer to the question about the Christian exemplar for man can be given in a single sentence. It can be expressed exhaustively in a single word: Christ."

I have suggested how Pieper's essay might be related to themes originated within contemporary moral philosophy by Anscombe; but I might equally have related it to ideas in social philosophy developed by critics of liberal individualism such as Alasdair MacIntyre and Charles Taylor, and to the developments in moral theology flowing from the influence of these three Anglophone Catholic thinkers. Yet while it may be useful to read Pieper with such others in mind, it is also important to read him on his account, in his own terms and with a view to learning the distinctive points he seeks to introduce. There is much to be got from the essay, not in the form of received doctrines but as suggestions about how we need to think about action and agency, value and nature, individual and society, aspiration and failure, about the ordering, integration, and degree of interdependence of the virtues, and much else besides.

Where the essay takes us to, however, is where it begins, not with a philosophical thesis but with a religious doctrine drawn from revelation: namely that human beings are created images of God, and on that account human virtue must look for its inspiration and strengthening to Christ and to "hope in the abundant reality of life, in eternal life, in a New Heaven and a New Earth." Pieper's essay can be read as a meditation or homily on a sentence from Aquinas: "Because man is created in the image of God it now remains – after His archetypal image has been dealt with – to speak of his reflection: namely man," but it also reads as an extended abstract for a treatise to be developed and adapted to the times in which it is read.

I hope that among those who may now read *The Christian Idea of Man* for the first time there will be some who will take up precisely that challenge, and offer an effective cultural and philosophical critique of the contemporary situation, along with ideas as to how to develop a theology of hope apt to our present condition.

John Haldane
St. Andrews
Scotland

The Christian Idea of Man

The Idea of Man in General

THE *SUMMA THEOLOGIAE*, WRITTEN BY THE "*DOCTOR Communis*," devotes the second part to moral theology. This part begins with the following sentence: "Because man is created as the image of God it now remains – after His archetypal image has been dealt with – to speak of his reflection: namely, man." Like so many sentences of St. Thomas Aquinas, the naturalness with which, without any fuss, this one is spoken can obscure the fact that its content is anything but obvious. This first sentence in his Moral Theology expresses an idea that we Christians of today have to some extent lost sight of: namely, that moral teaching is first and foremost teaching about man; that moral teaching must make the idea of man visible; and that therefore Christian moral teaching must deal with a Christian exemplar of man. This notion is something which Christendom in the High Middle Ages took for granted. From this obvious fundamental idea, which, of course, as the polemical formulation indicates, was already badly shaken, derives from Eckhart's statement two generations after Thomas Aquinas: people should not think so much about what they ought to do; they should think about what they ought to be. But later, for reasons which are difficult to fathom and are extraordinarily difficult to evaluate, moral theory and, above all, the proclamation of morality, has largely lost contact with this view, to such an extent that even moral theology textbooks written expressly "in the spirit of Saint Thomas" differ from him on this central point. Herein lie some of the reasons why the average Christian would not expect our moral and ethical teaching to tell us anything about the true being of man, about his true image. Instead, for us the concept of ethics is the teaching about doing and leaving undone, of being allowed and, above all, not being allowed, of what is commanded and, above all, what is forbidden.

And so that is the first teaching in the moral theology of the *"Doctor Communis"*: ethics is about the right conception of man. Naturally it is also concerned with doing, duties, commandments, and sins. But its primary object, which is the foundation of everything else, is: man's proper existence, the image of the good person.

The Christian Idea of Man and St. Thomas Aquinas's Theory of Virtues

THE ANSWER TO THE QUESTION ABOUT THE CHRISTIAN exemplar for man can be given in a single sentence. It can be expressed exhaustively in a single word: Christ. The Christian ought to be "another Christ"; he ought to be perfect like the father of Jesus Christ.

But this word about the perfection of the Christian, which encompasses simply everything and for that very reason can never be interpreted once and for all, needs to be unfolded, "applied"; it does need interpretation. Without such an interpretation beginning with the empirical essence of man and with reality, it would be constantly exposed to the danger of abuse and misunderstanding through a "short-circuit" which is not compatible with human existence. It is not possible, starting from the situation of concrete behavior, to have direct recourse to that highest and ultimate image and goal of perfection. The Fourth Lateran Council was referring precisely to the word of Scripture, "be perfect as your Heavenly Father is perfect" – and thus to the formulation of this most perfect Christian exemplar – with the famous sentence about the analogy of being: *Inter Creatorem et creaturam non potest tanta similitudo notari, quin inter eos maior sit dissimilitudo*, between the creator and the creature no similarity can be stated that would not require a statement of even greater dissimilarity between them. This sentence is directed against the idea of an all-too-immediate assimilation of man to the divinity. Man, even the Christian, even the perfect Christian, remains a creature, a finite being, even in eternal life.

Clearly there is more than one legitimate way of developing the interpretation of this ultimate Christian exemplar – not only from the theoretical but also from the historical point of view. For example, there is undoubtedly an East Christian and a West Christian (i.e. occidental) form of interpreting the Christian idea of man.

Thomas Aquinas, the great master of Western Christendom, decided to express the Christian idea of man in seven theses: First, the Christian is a person, who, in his *faith*, is aware of the reality

of the Trinity. Second, the Christian looks forward – in *hope* – to the ultimate fulfillment of his
being in eternal life. Third, the Christian – with
the Theological Virtue of *love* – turns to God and
his fellow man, affirming them with a love that is
far stronger than any natural love. Fourth, the
Christian is prudent, i.e. he does not let his view
of reality be clouded by what the will dictates
without reference to the truth about the real situation. Fifth, the Christian is just, i.e. he is able
to live in truth "with the other"; he sees that he
is one member among other members of the
Church, of the population, and of the all-embrac-
ing community. Sixth, the Christian is brave, i.e.
he is prepared to be harmed – and even to accept
death, if necessary – for truth and for the realization of justice. Seventh, the Christian is moder-
ate, i.e. he does not allow his desire for posses-
sions and enjoyment to become destructive and
repugnant to his being.

These seven theses mean that the ethics of
classical theology – insofar as it is a portrayal of
the idea of man – is essentially a theory of
the virtues; more precisely, it interprets the
biblical dictum about the perfection of the
Christian by reference to the three Theological
and the four Cardinal Virtues. And it is, I think, a

not unimportant task to bring back to general awareness the excellent original form of classical theology's idea of man, which has in many respects become faint and – worse still – many times painted over. Not for the sake of "historical" interest; not to ascertain and to show "how it really was"; but because this interpretation of the ultimate human exemplar has not only remained valid but because, as well, I believe, it is absolutely essential for our lives that we again see this idea of man clearly and that we affirm it.

I would now like to attempt, by way of some comments, to give an outline of this idea – especially with regard to the four Cardinal Virtues – in particular where it seems to me it has become faint or painted over.

The True Concept of Virtue and the Hierachy of the Virtues

FOR A START SOMETHING HAS TO BE SAID ABOUT THE concept of virtue itself. Some years ago at the French Academy an address was given about virtue by none other than Paul Valéry. He said: "Virtue, gentlemen, the word virtue is dead or is at least dying out. . . . For the contemporary mind it no longer serves as a direct expression of what we see as present day reality. . . . I must myself confess that I have never heard it, or rather – what is far more significant – I have always heard it mentioned only as a rarity and in an ironic sense when used in conversation in a normal social context. That could mean that I mix in the wrong circles – if I did not add that I do not remember encountering it in books which are currently the most read and the most highly prized. Finally, I know no newspaper that prints it or that would dare to print it, I fear, except for comical effect. So it has come to the point that the words 'virtue' and 'virtuous' can now only be found in the catechism, in jokes, in the Academy, and in comic opera."

This diagnosis by Paul Valéry is unquestionably correct. But one need not be very surprised. Partly this has to do with the completely natural phenomenon – the natural fate of the "great words." But then again, why would not, in a dechristianized world, the secularized (demonic) laws of language have their effect, so that in currently accepted speech the good appears as laughable? And finally – and above all – quite apart from this latter possibility, which is to be taken quite seriously, it should not be forgotten that Christian writing on, and promulgation of, morality has not always made it easy for the average man to grasp the genuine meaning of the concept and reality of "virtue."

Virtue does not mean "nice" and "orderly" behavior in relation to isolated instances of doing or leaving undone. Instead, virtue means that the person *is* right – in both the supernatural and natural sense. – Here there are two dangerous possibilities of perverting the concept of virtue within the general Christian awareness: first, the possibility of a moralistic attitude that isolates the doing, the execution, the practice, and absolutizes it over against the living existence of the living person; second, the possibility of a supernaturalism that devalues the realm of naturally healthy life, of vitality, of a naturally decent and clean existence.

And so virtue, in a quite general sense, raises the level of existence of the human person. Virtue is, as Thomas says, the *ultimum potentiae*; it is the ultimate of what a human person can be; it is the fulfillment of man's ability to *be* – in the natural and in the supernatural sphere. The virtuous person *is* in such a way that, from the innermost tendency of his being, he realizes the good through his actions.

Almost equally important as the correct concept of virtue is the insight into the order of importance among the virtues. There has often been talk of the "heroic" character of Christianity or of the "heroic" view of life as the fundamental aspect that distinguishes Christian life from that of others. These formulations are merely half-truths. The first and most distinctive virtue of the Christian is the supernatural love of God and neighbor. And the Theological Virtues, taken together, are of a higher order than the four Cardinal Virtues. Even my little book on the meaning of courage [*Vom Sinn der Tapferkeit*] has not escaped the half-true and half-false "heroistic" interpretation, although one of its main aims is to show that courage is not the first among the Cardinal Virtues, but the third.

Prudence

THE FIRST OF THE CARDINAL VIRTUES IS THE VIRTUE OF prudence. It is, indeed, not only the first of the virtues which are otherwise equal in rank: it "gives birth" to all moral virtue as such.

This dictum about the precedence of prudence, which we are scarcely able to grasp in its true meaning any longer, involves more than a more or less random sequence of Cardinal Virtues. It expresses, in relation to the sphere of the ethical, the fundamental way reality is constituted: good presupposes truth, and truth presupposes being. What is meant by the precedence of prudence? Only that realization of the good presupposes knowledge of reality. The first thing that is required of a person who acts is that he is aware, says Thomas. One who does not know how things really are cannot do good; for the good accords with reality. "Knowing," I hasten to add, is not to be taken in the scientific sense as understood by the modern empirical sciences. What is meant is: real contact with objective reality. This contact, through revelation, for example, is on a far better footing than a "scientific" one; and part of prudence is the eagerness to learn: i.e. the connection, through hearing, with the genuine knowledge of reality enjoyed by a superior mind. In prudence, objective knowledge of reality plays a decisive role for action. The prudent person looks, on the one hand, at the objective reality of things and, on the other hand, at will and action. But he looks first at reality; and by virtue of and on the basis of his knowledge of reality he decides what is to be done and what not, and how it is to be done and how not. And so in truth all virtue is dependent on prudence. And every sin is somehow in contradiction with prudence, *omne peccatum opponitur prudentiae.*

Our manner of speaking, which, as always, is also our manner of thinking, has become rather far removed from all this. Prudence seems to us to consist in avoidance of the good rather than in being a presupposition of the good. We find it very difficult to think that it is always and essentially "prudent" to be just and true. And indeed prudence and courage seem to be absolutely incompatible things: to be courageous is usually "imprudent."– But we have to remind ourselves that the true meaning here is the following: all just and courageous action, all good action at all, is just and courageous and good, because it corresponds to the divinely created truth in real things; and this truth contained in real things finds fruitful and definitive expression in the virtue of prudence.

This doctrine of the precedence of prudence has enormous "practical" significance. It implies, for example, the fundamental pedagogical principle: that education and self-education in ethical maturity must be rooted in education and the training of oneself in the virtue of prudence, i.e. in the ability to view objectively the realities surrounding our actions and making them have, depending on their kind and significance, a direct bearing on our actions.

In the classical teaching about the virtue of prudence lies also the only possibility of inwardly overcoming the repugnant phenomenon of moralism. The essence of moralism, which many think is something specially Christian, consists in the violent separation of being and duty from one another and in proclaiming something as obligatory without seeing and making visible its link to being. But the kernel and the real function of the doctrine of prudence is to show that there is a necessary link between obligation and being;

in the prudent action obligation is determined by being. Moralism says: good is what obligation requires, and because obligation requires it. The doctrine of prudence says: good is what accords with reality; it is obligatory because it corresponds to reality. (It is important to see clearly the inner connection which comes to light here between "Christian" moralism and modern voluntarism. Both of these phenomena are much more closely related with one another than appears at first sight.)

A third "practical" and "current" link must briefly be touched on here. The fundamental attitude that is at one with being and with objectivity, as expressed in the classical doctrine of prudence, was summed up in the medieval period in the wonderfully simple sentence: a man is wise if all things taste to him as they really are. It is, to my mind, an experience of modern psychology – or more precisely, of the modern psychology of healing – that can hardly be taken seriously enough: that a person to whom things do *not* taste as they are but who in all things tastes only himself because he has an eye only for himself – that this person has not only lost the real possibility of justice (and of any kind of moral virtue) but has also lost his mental health; and that the whole category of mental illnesses consists essentially in this self-centered non-objectivity. These experiences confirm and clarify the ethical realism of the theory of the precedence of prudence. Prudence is one of the spiritual points where the mysterious link between health and holiness, sickness and sin becomes visible. A psychology that does not deliberately choose to pass over these things will probably be able to see, from this starting point, very profound connections. The central characterological concept of self-deception (which is none other than an unobjective perception of reality dictated by the will) and, further, the quite parallel concept of "ideology" found in social theory, could be shown in a quite surprising light through the application of the ethical theory of prudence. But all of this can only be mentioned here in passing.

Justice

PRUDENCE AND JUSTICE ARE MORE CLOSELY CONNECTED than at first sight they would seem to be. Justice, we said, is the ability to live truly "with the other" (persons). But it is not difficult to see how much this art of living together – which almost amounts to saying: the art of living at all – is dependent on objective knowledge and acceptance of reality, and therefore on prudence. Only an objective person is just; and lack of objectivity means, also in ordinary everyday language, almost the same as injustice.

Prudence provides the real possibility of being good; only the prudent person has the presupposition required for being good. That is the reason why prudence rates so highly. Justice is to be rated highly because it is the highest and most genuine *form* of this being good. It is necessary to stress this after the "Christian" middle classes, for a number of generations, have held quite different things as the real and main characteristic of the good person: namely, his so-called "morality."

The good person is primarily just. It is not by chance that Holy Scripture and the liturgy of the Church characterize the man gifted with (divine) grace as "the just man." In dealing with this theme of "justice" even the otherwise completely sober teaching tone of St. Thomas tends to take wings; he quotes in his *Summa* Aristotle's dictum: "The most lofty of all virtues is justice; neither the morning star is worthy of such admiration, nor the evening star."

The practice of justice is required of man as a member of the community. It can almost be said that the one responsible for justice is not so much the individual (although, of course, only the person can be "virtuous" in the strict sense) as the "we," the social whole, the people; justice, therefore, completes the being of the "we." The structure of every single "we" is crystallized in three fundamental structural elements; and if these three structures are "right," one can then say: in this "we" justice reigns. These three structural elements are the following: first, the relations of the members to one another; the rightness of these relations concerns justice in exchange: commutative justice. Second, the relations of the whole to the members; the rightness of these relations concerns sharing out: distributive justice.

Third, the relations of the individual members to the "we" totality; the rightness of these relations corresponds – as the scholastics say – to "legal" justice. All these things *seem* very obvious, but they are not at all obvious.

The individualistic "social" theory, for example, looks at only one of these three fundamental structures, namely, the relations of the individuals to one another; individualism does not accept the genuine independence of the "we" totality and for this reason does not acknowledge any real relations of individuals to the totality or of the totality to the individuals. This means that the exchange relationship consisting in a contractual balancing of interests is the only form of justice recognized by individualism when it is consistent. Against this, anti-individualism has created a "universalist" social theory which flatly denies that there are any relations between individuals as individuals and which therefore, quite logically, declares that commutative justice is an "individualistic non-concept." How little these "schools of thought" tend to remain pure "theory" can be seen from what we have experienced of totalitarian regimes. These are characterized by the fact that the state, which can impose its will by force, leaves hardly any room for "private" relations between individuals as such, and that individuals encounter one another almost exclusively in an official capacity as individual functionaries serving the state.

In recent years, the attempt has been made from a Christian perspective to show the relationship of the individual to the common good of the "we" as the fundamental structural element of the life of the community, and thus to present "legal justice" as the true form of justice. It was also maintained simultaneously that this is the true meaning of classical theology. It is very difficult to make a correct judgment of this attempt since important and complex distinctions have to be made. Thomas Aquinas says indeed that the whole moral life of the person is related to the common good. For this reason legal justice really has a position of quite considerable importance. But it must not be overlooked that this thesis of St. Thomas has two sides to it. One side is that it expresses the individual's genuine obligation to the common good, and this obligation affects the whole person. But the other side is this: all virtue of the individual is of considerable importance for the common good, which means that the common good needs the virtue of all individuals; it is not achievable if the individual members of the community are not good – not only "just" in the narrow sense, but "good," even in the sense of the most personal and hidden, and, so to speak, most private virtue.

Courage and Fear of the Lord

THERE IS ANOTHER ERROR CONCERNING JUSTICE. Basically it is a liberalist error, but it is not confined to the so-called "Age of Liberalism." It is this: one can be just without needing to be courageous. This is not so much an error about the nature of justice but a wrong conception of the way "this" world, in which justice has to be realized, is constituted in being. "This" world is so constructed that justice, like every kind of good, does not "of itself" "succeed" without a personal commitment that includes willingness to face death. Evil has power in "this" world: this fact is clear from the necessity of courage, which is none other than the readiness to accept harm for the sake of realizing the good. As St. Augustine says, courage is itself incontrovertible testimony to the existence of evil in the world.

Now it is a bad and likewise wrong response to the liberalist error to think it is possible to be courageous without being just. Courage is only virtue where justice is the aim. One who is not just cannot in a genuine sense be courageous. St. Thomas says: "Praise of courage depends on justice." That means that I can only praise a person for his courage if I can at the same time also praise him for his justice. True courage is therefore essentially connected with the will to be just.

It is no less important to realize that the idea of courage is not identical with the idea of aggressive fearlessness. There is even a fearlessness which contradicts the virtue of courage. To achieve a clearer picture of this one needs to consider what place is occupied by fear in the make-up of human existence.

The foreground "talk" of daily life, essentially aimed at reassurance, is nourished from the denial that the terrible exists or from relegating it as unreal and the untrue. This process of reassurance, effective (or not) in all ages, is today remarkably countered by the fact that, in the background, in the philosophical, psychological, and creative writing of our time, there is no concept that plays a role comparable with that played by the concept of fear.

Another opponent of this daily playing down of fear in our existence is the new stoicism, proclaimed, above all, by a circle of men for whom the events of the world wars are remembered as a destruction which carries within it the promise and threat of still more monumental and apocalyptic catastrophes. Everywhere existence is awful, but there is nothing so awful that the strong man cannot, in his greatness, take it on his shoulders and endure it. But if you read the more personal books of Ernst Jünger, for example – who is one of the most remarkable minds of the new Stoa – you notice that nearly all the dreams of these "adventurous hearts" are nightmares. Here it should be noted that it would not only be entirely ludicrous to view this fact with some sort of "smugness" or even irony. These nightmares are an answer to the true metaphysical situation in the West – an answer which is both humanly greater and perhaps objectively more in accordance with reality than the answer of a Christianity which is satisfied with previous "cultural" certainties and which has not yet managed to achieve contact with its own depths. In these depths lies the ultimate Christian answer in this context: it is the concept of *fear of the Lord.* But this concept, emptied of the Christian consciousness of community, is in the process of being stripped of reality and obscured. Fear of the Lord is not simply the same as "respect" for the absolute God, but real fear in the strict sense of the word. What words like fear [*Furcht, Angst*], fright [*Schrecken*], horror [*Grauen, Entsetzen*] have in common is that they are all answers to the different forms of diminution of our being, the most extreme of which would be our actual destruction. Christian theology would in no way deny that there are terrible experiences in human existence; Christian teaching is also far from maintaining that, for example, man should not or may not fear the terrible. But the Christian asks about the *ordo timoris*, the hierarchy of fear; he asks what is really and ultimately terrible; and he is concerned not to fear things which are not really and ultimately terrible, and he is concerned not to judge as harmless what is the ultimately terrible. The ultimately terrible is none other than the possibility that the person, through guilt, willingly separates himself from the ultimate ground of being. The possibility of incurring guilt is the most extreme danger to human existence. And fear of the Lord is the appropriate answer to the fearsomeness of the ever-possible separation, in guilt, from the ultimate foundation of being. Guilt is what is ultimately terrible. No one can bear it and take it upon himself "with greatness." This fearsomeness, which accompanies every human existence as a real possibility –

even the existence of a saint – this fearsomeness and this fear cannot be overcome by any form of "heroism"; this fear is, on the contrary, the presupposition for all genuine heroism. Fear of the Lord – as fear – has to be borne and endured until the ultimate "certainty" of eternal life. If courage protects us from loving our life in such a way that we lose it – that means that fear of the Lord as fear of the loss of *eternal* life is the foundation of all Christian courage. One must, of course, keep in mind that fear of the Lord is only the negative side of hope in, and love of, God. Augustine says: All fear is love that flees.

In fear of the Lord the natural fear man has of diminution and annihilation of his being reaches "completion." All that is morally good is nothing but a kind of "prolongation" of natural tendencies of being. But man has a "natural" fear of nothingness – prior to all intellectual decisions – which means: according to his God-given nature. Now, just as the natural drive to live in society reaches perfection in the virtue of justice; and just as the natural drive to self-aggrandizement reaches its perfection in magnanimity; and just as the natural desire for enjoyment reaches perfection in the virtue of moderation – so the natural fear of annihilation reaches perfection in: fear of the Lord.

And just as these natural drives become destructive if they do not reach fulfillment in justice, magnanimity, and moderation – so the natural fear of annihilation becomes destructive if it does not find fulfillment in fear of the Lord. The fact that fear of the Lord, in its proper form as "filial" fear, is a gift of the Holy Spirit, and therefore unlike the Cardinal Virtues, for instance, is not the natural moral fulfillment of natural human possibilities of being – this fact means that only really lived supernatural perfection can free man completely from the tyranny of "unfulfilled" fear.

Incidentally, the destructive effect of this "unfulfilled" fear and its tyranny is to be seen not just in the ethical sphere but also in the sphere of the natural life of the mind and soul. In this respect psychiatry can be informative. Here again is a point where the relationship between health and holiness becomes apparent. What is clear, of course, is merely the *fact* of the connection. Precisely *how* health and holiness, and, above all, guilt and sickness, are inwardly linked with one another, and under what conditions this link comes about – it is hardly possible to say. In any case, the "health" of justice, magnanimity, moderation, fear of the Lord, and of any virtue at all is to be found in the fact that they accord with objective reality – both natural and supernatural. Correspondence with reality is, at one and the same time, the principle of health and the good.

Discipline and Moderation

WE HAVE BEEN SAYING HERE THAT THE NATURAL DRIVE for enjoyment can become destructive. This truth is obscured by the liberalist thesis that "man is good." Enlightened liberalism could not, because of its fundamental presuppositions, acknowledge in man the possibility of a rebellion – a rebellion which is repugnant to his being – by the subordinate powers of the soul against the rule of the spirit. It denies that man through original sin has lost the natural inner order within himself. It follows quite logically that in this scheme of things the virtue of moderation is seen as intrinsically meaningless, contrary to all good sense, and invalid. The virtue of moderation presupposes that the destructive rebellion of the senses against the spirit – which is repugnant to being – is possible and is recognized as such. The answer given by Christianity in latter generations (I do not say: the teaching of the Church. I do not even say: theology) to this removal of meaning from the virtue of moderation by enlightened

liberalism has been a specially accentuated high-
lighting of precisely this virtue; the virtue of moderation, in its typical forms of chastity and absti-
nence, became in the Christian mind *the* most
prominent characteristic of the Christian idea of
man and one that dominated everything else. Yet
this answer of Christendom nevertheless
remained quite dependent on its liberalist and
individualistic opponent. This dependence is
shown in the fact that the virtue of moderation is
the most "private" of the four Cardinal Virtues.
There is no reason why the banner of the virtue
of courage could not just as well have been
unfurled against enlightened liberalism; or –
quite apart from distributive and legal justice –
the virtues of courage and moderation could have
been given special prominence and proclaimed;
for, by its absolute optimism about earthly existence, liberalism had hollowed out the founda-
tions of *both* virtues, both of which presuppose
the existence of evil. But – again, in the general
consciousness of Christendom! – precisely the
virtue of moderation was put forward as *the* characteristic Christian virtue; the virtue which, as
we have said, relates first of all to the individual
as individual. Thus the most private virtue was
taken to be the most Christian. In this way the

overvaluing of moderation is quite closely related to liberalism – through the privatizing of the ethical. For classical theology, on the other hand, the private character of moderation is the reason for saying that this virtue is not the first but precisely the last of the four Cardinal Virtues.

It hardly needs to be mentioned that here nothing is being said against the dignity and necessity of discipline and moderation, nothing against the shining validity of purity. It is also not being contested that, in a world characterized by a shallow pursuit of pleasure, special importance must be attached to education – and to educating oneself to honorableness. It is a question of the essential ranking of the moral virtues in accordance with the idea of the "good" person.

Overvaluing moderation in principle has radiated quite considerable effects. First, this is where the concept of so-called "morality" has its roots. This concept as it is now used in everyday speech and with all its ambiguous connotations is the result, on the one hand, of limiting the ethical to mean the virtue of moderation, and is combined, on the other hand, with a moralistic conception of the good, a conception which, as was said above, isolates the (act of) "performance" or omission from the person and forcibly separates duty and being.

Furthermore, something which is rarely adverted to, the exemplary and powerfully impressive force, for example, of the angel or the Mother of God, is claimed one-sidedly for this aspect of virtue, especially for chastity. The result has been that these figures have not remained present in the general Christian consciousness in the full richness of their reality. With regard to the concept of "angelic purity," it should be noted that an angel cannot at all be "pure" in the sense implied by the virtue of chastity, and that the virtuousness of the angel lies first and foremost in the Theological Virtue of love. In the same way, the concept of the *Immaculata* refers to something much more comprehensive than the chastity of the Mother of God; it means, above all, to the fullness of being and grace which was given to Mary from the beginning.

Finally, the overvaluation of moderation is not entirely without blame for the fact that in our use of language the words "sensuality" [*Sinnlichkeit*], "passion," "desire," "drive," etc., have acquired a thoroughly negative meaning, although they designate what are, to begin with, ethically neutral concepts. But if our use of language takes "sensuality" exclusively to mean something repugnant to spirit, "passion" to be exclusively an evil passion, and "desire" to be exclusively rebellious desire, then there are no names left to signify the kind of sense life that is neither repugnant nor rebellious to spirit. St. Thomas says that this latter sense life is part of virtue. And the deficit in our use of language brings about only too easily a dangerous confusion of concepts, even of life itself – just as, on the other hand, the weakness in language usage itself derives from a confusion of concepts and confusion in life.

It is perhaps good to cite here an example from St. Thomas's *Summa Theologiae* which shows how the *"Summa Communis"* thinks in this matter; it is an example, not a principle, but an example that sheds light on a principle. In the *Summa* there is a tract about the *passiones animae*, the passions of the soul. Thomas understands them to mean all the stirrings of our faculty of sense, of desire: for instance, love, hate, desire, pleasure, sadness, fear, anger, etc. One of the some twenty-five Questions of this tract deals with "the remedies against pain and sadness." Thomas presents in five separate articles as many such remedies. But before we look at them, let us keep in mind the question: what information would, or even *could*, the general moral consciousness of today's Christendom give about "remedies against sadness of the soul"? This question each one can answer for himself. The first, quite general remedy that Thomas mentions is: "any kind of pleasure," for sadness is a weariness of the soul, whereas pleasure is like rest. Second remedy: tears! Third remedy: the sympathy of friends. Fourth: contemplating the truth; it soothes the pain the more completely the person loves wisdom. With regard to the fifth remedy that Thomas names, we must remind ourselves that what we have in front of us is not just any kind of book but a manual of *theology*. So: the fifth remedy against sadness is taking a sleep and a bath; for these bring the body its due sense of well-being, which in turn reacts on the soul! Naturally Thomas knows very well about the possibility and necessity of the *supernatural* answer to human suffering; he is even of the opinion that there are forms and levels of human suffering that can *only* be borne in the supernatural. But Thomas is in no way inclined to omit the natural and sense possibilities – for example, sleeping and bathing. And he is not in the least embarrassed to speak about it in the middle of his theology.

Faith, Hope, and Love

THIS ENDS THE SERIES OF COMMENTS ABOUT THE Cardinal Virtues. All four of them – prudence, justice, courage, and moderation – relate in the first instance to the natural sphere of human reality. But, as Christian virtues, they grow out of the fruitful soil of faith, hope, and love.

Faith, hope, and love are the response to the reality of the Divine Trinity which has been revealed to the Christian in a supernatural way through the revelation of Jesus Christ. And, furthermore, the three Theological Virtues are not only the response to this reality, but they are at the same time the capacity and source of strength needed to make this response; they are not just the answer, they are also, so to speak, the mouth which alone is capable of making this answer. This fact does not emerge clearly enough in all Christian utterances about the Theological Virtues. It is not the case that, once the supernatural reality has been made, so to speak, "accessible," natural man can of himself – merely "by hearing about it" – "believe" in the sense intrinsic to the Theological Virtue of "faith." No, this possibility of "believing" does not come about except through the communication of grace, which makes the person holy.

In faith the Christian becomes aware of the reality of the Divine Trinity in a way which transcends all natural awareness. Hope is the answer – given by God to the Christian in his inner existence – to the revealed fact that Christ, in the most real sense of the word, is the "Way" to eternal life. Finally, love is – in accord with the reality of things – the answer given by all the powers of affirmation enjoyed by man, in grace,– to the inexhaustible lovable reality that is God. All three Theological Virtues are inextricably connected with one another; they "flow," as Thomas says in his tract about hope, "back into themselves in a holy circle; one who was led to love through hope also has from now on more perfect hope, just as his faith is now stronger than before."

The Distinction between a Natural and Supernatural Ethos

SINCE THE CARDINAL VIRTUES ARE ROOTED IN THE Theological Virtues, the supernatural ethos of the Christian is distinguished from the natural ethos of the *gentleman*, the naturally noble man.

This rootedness itself, the kind of connection that links natural and supernatural virtue, is expressed in the well-known dictum that grace does not destroy nature but presupposes and perfects it. This sentence seems clear, and it is. But its clarity does not remove the impossibility of making a mystery comprehensible by means of a statement. And nothing is richer in mystery than the way God is at work in man and man is at work in God.

In spite of this the difference between the Christian and the *gentleman* has manifold aspects which are tangible enough.

The Christian can, for example, appear to act

in a way that is repugnant to natural prudence, because in his actions he has to do justice to a reality of which only faith is aware. – Incidentally, Thomas Aquinas has written something about this "supernatural prudence" which seems to me extremely important for a Christian today. The natural virtue of prudence, says St. Thomas, is obviously tied to a not-insignificant measure of knowledge of reality. But if the Theological Virtues elevate the natural virtues in a supernatural way, what is to be said of prudence? Does grace replace natural knowledge about natural things? Does faith make the objective appraisal of the concrete situation of our concrete actions superfluous, or replace it? What use is grace and faith to the "ordinary man" who does not possess this sometimes difficult concrete knowledge? Thomas answers these questions with what is, to my mind, a quite superb and also very consoling response: "People who need to be led and advised by others can, when they are living in grace, make up their own minds about asking other people's advice and are able to distinguish between good and bad advice." When they are living in grace! In what way this answer is consoling in the present situation in which the "simple Christian" finds himself needs no further elaboration.

There is an especially striking distinction between the Christian and the *gentleman* in the distance which separates Christian courage from the natural courage of the *gentleman*. And here we are to conclude our thoughts about the Christian idea of man. The distinction between Christian and purely natural courage resides ultimately in the Theological Virtue of hope. Hope of every kind says: it will work out well, all will be well in the end. Supernatural hope says: for the man who exists in the divine reality of grace it will end in a way that infinitely exceeds all expectation; for such a person it will end with no less a thing than eternal life. But it can happen that in a time when there are temptations to despair all inner-worldly prospects of a "happy ending" will grow dim, and so it can happen that for the man who is limited to the natural sphere there is nothing left except the hopeless courage of a "heroic downfall." And this possibility will present itself precisely to the genuine *gentleman* as the only one: for precisely he will be the one who knows how to renounce the reassuring self-deception and anesthetic and, as Ernst Jünger says, "the escape route of happiness." In a word, it can therefore come about that supernatural hope is simply the only possible hope that is left. This is not meant in some sort of eudemonistic sense; here we are not dealing with worry about the ultimate possibility of subjective happiness. The word of Holy Scripture, "Even if He kills me I will hope in Him," is worlds apart from eudemonistic fear for happiness. No, Christian hope is first and foremost an existential orientation of man to his fulfillment in being, to the fulfillment of his essence, to his ultimate fulfillment, to the fullness of existence (to which, of course, the fullness of happiness – or rather, bliss – corresponds). If therefore, as we have said, all natural kinds of hope become meaningless for the person the only possibility that remains is one's orientation to being. The despairing courage of the "heroic downfall" is fundamentally nihilistic, it is staring at nothingness; it thinks it can stand up to nothingness. But the courage of the Christian is nourished from hope in the abundant reality of life, in eternal life, in a New Heaven and a New Earth.

Index

angel(s), 33
Anscombe, Elizabeth, ix,
    xi–xii; "Modern Moral
    Philosophy," ix–x
anthropology: philosophi-
    cal, ix; theological, ix
Aquinas, Thomas, xi, xiii,
    3–4, 6, 11, 19, 21, 24,
    34–35, 38, 40; *Summa
    Theologiae*, 3, 19, 34
Arendt, Hannah, viii
Aristotle, 19
Augustine, St., 23, 27

Cardinal Virtues, 7–8, 11–
    13, 28, 31–32, 37–38;
    as rooted in the
    Theological Virtues,
    39. *See also* prudence,
    justice, courage, mod-
    eration.
Catholic Church, viii
chastity, 33
Christian exemplar:
    Christ as, xii, 3, 5–6, 8

Cologne People's Daily,
    viii
consequentialism, x
courage, 7, 23–29; natural
    v. Christian courage,
    40; as occasioning
    the perfection of the
    natural drive to self–
    aggrandizement, 27
creature, man as, 6

desire, 33–34
duty, x

Eckhart, Meister, 4
evil, 23, 31

faith, 6, 38, 40
fear and fearlessness, 24,
    26–27; hierarchy of
    fear, 26; and fear of
    the Lord, 25–28: as
    loss of eternal life, 27:
    as the negative of hope,
    27: as occasioning the

perfection of the natu-
ral fear of annihilation,
27–28. *See also*
courage
Fourth Lateran Council, 6

gentleman, v. Christian,
39, 41
God (the Father), 5
good life, living the, xi
good, as seen through
actions, 11; as being
in accord with reality,
16–17
grace, 19, 40; living in
grace, 40; grace per-
fecting nature, 39
guilt, 26
Gurian, Waldemar vii–viii

Haldane, John, vi–xiv
happiness, human, vii
Holy Spirit, 28
hope, 7, 38, 41–42

ideology, 17
individualism, ix, 31

Jesus Christ, 37
Jünger, Ernst, 25, 41–42
justice, 7, 18–22, 28; as
the art of living togeth-
er, 18; commutative

(between individuals),
19–21; distributive
(between the whole
and its members),
19–22; "legal justice"
(between individuals
and the "we" totality),
20–21, 23; as occa-
sioning the perfection
in the natural drive to
live in society, 27

liberalism, ix, 30–32; and
liberalist error (to
think it is possible to
be courageous within
being just), 23, 30–31
love, 7, 33, 38; of God and
neighbor, 11

MacIntyre, Alasdair, xii
magnanimity. *See*
courage.
Maritain, Jacques, viii
Mary (mother of Jesus), 33
moderation, 7, 28, 30–36;
as occasioning the per-
fection of the natural
desire for enjoyment,
27; overvaluing moder-
ation, 32–34
moral philosophy, x–xi,
3–4

Index

moral teaching: as teaching about man, 3
moralism, 10, 15–16; defined: 15

norms, xi

objective knowledge: as necessary for the realization of the good, 13; as necessary for prudence, 14
obligation, moral, x–xi
original sin, 30

passion, 33–34
Philosophy, ix
philosophy, xi,
Pieper, Josef, vii–xiv
prohibition, x–xi
prudence, 7, 13–18, 40
psychology, philosophy of, x
purity, 32

Rawls, John, x

sadness, remedy for 34–35
Scheler, Max, viii

self–deception, 17
sensuality, 34
Sidgwick, Henry, x–xi; *Methods of Ethics, The*, x
social philosophy, xii
species man, xi
stoicism, 24–25
supernaturalism, 11

Taylor, Charles, xii
The Review of Politics, vii
Theological Virtues, 7, 11, 37–40. *See also* faith, hope, love.
theology, xi, 7,
Trinity, 7, 37–38

utilitarianism, x

Valery, Paul, 9–10
virtue ethics, vii
virtue and virtues, ix, xi, xiii, 7, 9–10; virtue as being right, 10; hierarchy of virtues, 11
Voegelin, Eric, viii
voluntarism, 165

will, 17